MIKE AND DEBBY BIVIN

COM MON GROUND

FINDING SACRED SPACE IN YOUR MARRIAGE

Common Ground

Acknowledgements

Mike:

Man-o- man, there is no way to express the gratitude and thanks to Elizabeth "Doc" Gorden and Anastasia Wessner and a host of others. Doc is the one who took our - well my - scribble scrabble, run-on sentences that would and do run to infinity and beyond and placed them in a format you could read without needing oxygen and, somehow - hahaha - kept our voice. She and her man Samuel "Commish" Gorden are huge blessings in our lives.

Stasia took our initial, second, and third drafts and provided much-needed insight to add some clarity where needed and encouraged us to offer examples, illustrations to help provide "me too" moments. She has a gift that I'm thankful she is willing to share with us and that's herself. High fives to you both!

Then there was a weekend when 6 other couples dared to come together. A cross section of ages and length of years in marriage. The first night was spent dining, connecting hearts through and then Saturday happened.

An incredible Saturday morning into the early evening was spent with a group of people molding, praying, laughing, and fine tuning this book with statements like "What did you mean here?" "This would flow better in the next chapter" or "Uh, this needs to be canned." Transparency, honesty abounded as we knew our common ground was and is Jesus Christ. Thanks to Michael & Mary Katherine Jordan, Paul & Kelly Hurley, Jordan & April Crenshaw, Jon & Rita Robertson, Steve & Wendy Buchanan, and Doc & Commish Gorden.

Finally, there is this group of people in our lives, (too many to list as I will leave some out by accident), that have determined to beLIeVE a life that is transparent, mask free. It is a people who create an environment that is a refuge wherever we are - especially on Tuesday nights in our home and on Sunday evenings at the walNUT house. It's a people who are damming the torpedoes at "I'm fine" and daringly sharing their lives in a wide ass open fashion that would scare most of the "church goers," yet I believe was how our 1st century brothers and sisters beLIeVED life. For years the tears and belly laughs we share have a depth that can only be experienced when you know your identity, therefore you allow yourself the time to journey with fellow sojourners who know that their circumstances don't determine their identity, but our identity is set in CHRIST and CHRIST alone. Thank you to all who have ever been willing to hang out with my little bald head. You are loved.

Debby:

There is no way that any of this could even be possible without the HUGE GOD in our story together. It's because of the trials on our journey together and the hands on experience we have had together that this has even been possible. One thing I do know is this: a thriving, joy-filled, crazy love marriage is found with Christ as the foundation and a ton of meeting one another in the middle. I am crazy in love with the ONE who has redeemed our marriage and our story.

I am super thankful for my man, the one who loves my heart well, tells me he loves me over and over because he knows I need it, emulates Jesus in the flesh every day, and seeks to honor me by the way he loves me OUT LOUD every day. We are stronger because of the common ground we seek to share every day. I love you, Mike Bivins.

Mike (again):

Love you my little brown-eyed girl!

Introduction

"It was 700 fence posts from your place to ours. Neither one of us was old enough to drive a car. Sometimes it was rainin' and sometimes it would shine. We wore out that gravel road between your house and mine." [1]

Not sure where you were when this amazing song by Diamond Rio flashed onto the scene back in 1991. I was 27 years old and had been married for a whopping two years to this spark plug of a girl from Humboldt, TN. I was making my big splash into corporate America and wondering why no one had won the race yet. You know, the rat race. I thought I had to climb the 'ole corporate ladder, since the first of our three children was on the way in November. I didn't have a clue how to be a husband, much less a daddy! But the words to this song would linger back to me at some of the craziest times. Take a peek at the words in the chorus:

"I'd start walking your way/You'd start walking mine/We'd meet in the middle/'Neath that old Georgia pine/We'd gain a lot of ground/'Cause we'd both give a little/There ain't no road too long/When we meet in the middle"

We'd gain a lot of ground (love that) because we'd BOTH give a little, and when you and your spouse do, there is this sweet place called Common Ground. It's a place where those of us reading these pages before marriage would surrender our "have to have it my way" Burger King mentality to "Why, it's whatever you want, dear." It's that place when you couldn't wait for the phone on the wall to ring, the phone that had 40 ft. cord attached so you could build a labyrinth trail to a place where you would whisper into each other's being until one of you fell asleep. It's that place before careers, work, hobbies, school, bars, sports, and kids when you sought out each other first instead of last. It's the place of laughter and dreams happily ever after.

You see, Debby and I still believe in happily ever after and we believe you do too, or you would have never started walking towards each other. You would have never walked that aisle, beachside, courthouse, drive-through Vegas wedding chapel or that backyard with the 700 fence posts to where you said I DO. This book will help you start walking and, more importantly, help you discover each other all over again. You will be able to discover and understand some of the decisions that allowed the "world" to take control of your lives. You will learn how to STOP, DROP, AND PRAY through conversations that find you at odds (and you will). Best of all, for those who are willing to gain a lot of ground "cause [you'd] both give a little" is that you will discover the beauty of having our bridegroom Jesus Christ at the center of your marriage.

You don't have to be married in order to benefit from the information listed in these pages. All relationships have some of the same traits in regards to how we communicate with each other. The majority of the text will center on how to navigate through a marriage in how you chat with one another. Some of the same tips we provide that create awareness of where you are in the relationship can and will help in all type of friendships, including those in the work environment, in school, and in homes.

Before we dive into the deep end…let me introduce you to who you are chatting with. Hello from Mike and Debby Bivins!

Yep that's us…married, hitched, tied the knot on March 11, 1989. We have 4 children: Tanner (in heaven, more on him in a bit)…Kinsey (Gulley; Kek), our oldest daughter, is married to Bryan Johnson. Kinsey is an educator in our local school system and her man Bryan slams out work at high levels in Nashville, TN. Madison (ML; Madi Leigh), our middle child, is attending Middle Tennessee State University, where she is studying Psychology and a member of a sorority. Michael (Biv), our youngest, is 16 and will be entering his junior year of high school in the fall of 2016. Michael is part of the soccer team, loves to fish, and enjoys skateboards of all sizes. All of our kiddos love to laugh and have a blast in the great outdoors. They genuinely enjoy being with each other.

Chapter 1
How Did We Get Here?

No one ever tells you that the choices you make when you are younger, with little care and less responsibility, might just follow you when you are trying to build a foundation of marriage, chase a career, and make a family. No one tells you that the "harmless fun" of partying until you pass out, can't remember how you got home after mindlessly puking in the bushes, or grabbing your girlfriend and squeezing her so tightly that it makes her afraid that you're going to hurt her, that these things would attach themselves to you for more than 15 years like a cancer that devours and seeks to destroy.

Like a piece of glass that's embedded in your heel when you're a kid, you just adjust your step so you can still walk, still function, and no one else will notice the pain you feel, so that you can move through life and no one will ask "What's wrong?", a mask firmly was attached to my identity. I lived the life of a functional co-addict to an alcoholic for the first 12 years of our marriage.

The free-spirited fun of the party life isn't so much fun anymore when you get up in the middle of the night to a baby who needs you, only to wake early to parent and teach 25 Kindergarteners for seven hours, then to come home to a man who already had a 6 pack before he got home, unbeknownst to you, and continued to drink until he passed out. Every single day. So the coping mechanisms started. Pretending, silence, anger, nagging, isolation, and withholding sex (which wasn't that often because he was habitually passed out in our mauve recliner from exhaustion from his job and Miller Lites).

And there was a time that we felt the work it took to keep us afloat in marriage seemed more than the energy either one of us had. We are so thankful that we always knew that we loved one another and were for one another and that made the hard work it took to make our marriage thrive so worth it.

There are defining moments in our lives when we wake up and think "How in the world did I get here? I didn't sign up for this, and I'm not sure I even want this!" The world today looks around and says, "Why marriage? What's the use?"

Our purpose through these pages is to help discover or re-discover your purpose, your why back when you said yes to each other. And in doing so you will find out how to beLIeVE WIDE OPEN and in that, beLIeVING love will flow through you to your spouse, significant other, friends, relatives, co-workers. Yet you have to beLIeVE you are worthy to give and receive the aforementioned love.

Have you noticed?

Are you asking yourself "why are you capitalizing LIVE with the word believe?

To beLIeVE simply means to **live** out who you believe you are. When harsh or affirming words penetrate your heart you will start to beLIeVING that you are "less than" which will eventually turn your spouse into an enemy. When, in fact, it's THE enemy that is trying to do what he has been doing since the garden when Adam and Eve ate the fruit, and that is to separate.

The enemy's number 1 play in relationships especially marriage is silence. Yep if he can get us to stop sharing how we truly feel in the moment, the silence will turn to bitterness, resentment, and anger.

It's the same silence that penetrated Adam and Eve in the garden. God is speaking and paradise is formed. He then places the man (Adam) in the garden to tend and watch over it. He is coaching up Adam, giving him instructions and in particular says
(LET ME KNOW IF YALL THINK THIS FITS Or toss it)

Genesis 2:16 NLT *But the Lord God warned him, "you may freely eat the fruit of every tree in the garden---EXCEPT (capital for emphasis) the tree of knowledge of good and evil. If you eat it's fruit, are sure to die."*

Don't know about yall, but that would at least have me looking at that tree a few times. I'm remembering where the tree is, uh Lord what did you call that tree, remembering the leaves, the bark....attaching death to eating it...blazed in memory.

Adam then receives a wonderful and beautiful gift in the form of Eve, his bride. I believe it's safe to say that Adam had given Eve the same tour of the garden that God had given him, and as they were strolling through Adam pointed out the tree. Yea, don't you think he told her

Adam: "Look Eve this tree, this tree of knowledge, it's off limits, we are not to eat of this tree ok?"

Eve: "sure, but why?"..."what's up with the fruit on this tree?"

Adam: "God said we can have all of it except this one, that the fruit from this tree would bring death. Eve he said we would surely die if we eat it's fruit"

The serpent appears (Genesis 3) and we know the rest of the story...the enemy casts doubt.

There had to be this moment of silence between Adam and Eve before they ever crunched on the fruit...the enemy had slithered in to create and separate through the silence.

Through the pages you will learn to overcome silence in your relationship, you will learn to remind the enemy that we are operating from VICTORY. Victory over death handed to us through our beLIeVING Jesus Christ.

Let's remind the enemy that we are operating from a place of victory and we will no longer be silent.

 DIGGIN' IN:

What are some words you speak over yourself or have allowed to be spoken over you?

Some examples:
- You are not enough.
- You're worthless.
- You're wrong.
- You're too much.
- What were you thinking?
- You are hopeless.
- You'll never change.

Who does Jesus say you are?

Do you beLIeVE Him?

If you're not sure who you are in Christ, then it's impossible to live from the place of authority He provides.

Who we are

- You are holy and without blame before Him in love (Ephesians 1:4; 1 Peter 1:16)

- You are alive with Christ (Ephesians 2:5)
- You have received the gift of righteousness and reign as a king in life by Jesus Christ (Romans 5:17).
- You have the mind of Christ (1 Corinthians 2:16; Philippians 2:5)
- You have the Greater One living in me; greater is He Who is in me than he who is in the world (1 John 4:4).
- You are God's workmanship, created in Christ unto good works (Ephesians 2:10
- You can do all things through Christ Jesus (Philippians 4:13).
- You are a new creature in Christ (2 Corinthians 5:17).
- You are a spirit being alive to God (Romans 6:11; 1 Thessalonians 5:23).
- You are a believer, and the light of the Gospel shines in my mind (2 Corinthians 4:4).
- You are a joint-heir with Christ (Romans 8:17).
- You are more than a conqueror through Him Who loves me (Romans 8:37)
- You are an ambassador for Christ (2 Corinthians 5:20)

You will find so many more in The Book (Bible). Grab your favorite search engine, type in "who I am in Christ verses," print them off, and place them in areas of your home. Drink 'em in! Also, you can check out the back of this book for more, taken from Neil Anderson's *Victory over Darkness*.

This is vital: as we will move in our lives, we will function from a place of knowing who and whose we are. Meaning, we will live out who we believe we are in each interaction. If your inner voice of "I'm a loser" is louder than the Voice of Christ saying you are God's workmanship, your life will manifest (beLIeVE)"I'm a loser."

Does this connect for you? In other words, if you don't know who you are in Christ, then you will raise others in your life up to determine your value. Thus, beLIeVING in that moment you are who that person says you are versus who Christ says you are.

Debby and I get the chance to sit with individuals and couples weekly. It's not the typical 'go into an office' setting where the couple or individual is tighter than a banjo string being in a place they never thought they would be. I'm not necessarily talking about the physical place of an office, but the place of being in the same room with your spouse when bitterness, anger, or resentment is coursing through. This is a place you never thought you would be when you said "I do."

Debby and I desire to live life with folks in our home, around a table in a coffee shop, or in the homes of others. That's really where life happens, right? In doing so, we find people are a bit more relaxed, and then we help them know they are in a safe place by telling them our story straight from our hearts. We get a chance to hear their stories and some of their backgrounds. Inevitably, pain (emotional injury) has entered the relationship through the door of some wound in their past that hasn't quite healed. It manifests in lies (untruths) that they beLIeVE about themselves, lies that turn into self-worth, image, and self-condemnation.

They simply will not allow themselves at times to beLIeVE that God through Jesus Christ blew life into them on purpose.

It reminds me when we ask couples to take a look at their hands. To look at the top and then turn them over and take a big long look at their palms and fingers. Ah, so while we are here go ahead, take a look at your hands, the lines, the ridges running through them. "What's unique about them" is the question we ask.

What's your answer? YES, your fingerprints! The creator of planets, galaxies, and even solar systems we have yet to discover beLIeVED it necessary to blow life into you. What is your birth date? Get this (give me a little wiggle room here - illustration for emphasis) God the Father, Jesus, and the Holy Spirit are on the scene and deciding who will be born, deciding, discussing "Hey you know what we need a Michael Bivins" and on June 8, 1964, I was plucked out of eternity to beLIeVE. They continue: "Yeah, yeah, yeah! We need - not only need but want - Debra Sue Nicodemus" so on July 20, 1966, my bride was plucked out of eternity to beLIeVE. Isn't that amazingly cool? AND AND AND. God being so deliberate in how he blows life into us, he wanted to make sure you were never mistaken for someone else, thus the reason for your very own identifiers in your fingerprints, your dental, heck your DNA. NO ONE has yours! There are over 7 billion individuals with their own DNA! That, my friends, is an ON purpose GOD!

beLIeVING this will be your first step in healing and creating a marriage that will be WIDE OPEN fun.

As you are looking at your hands, draw the lines to help demonstrate your uniqueness. When finished compare with your spouse. Do you have any lines that match or similar? So just as your uniqueness is not lost in the marriage, the coming together of your uniqueness creates a DNA within your marriage that is like no one else…you we are one of kind through the ONE.

QUICK FACT

Did you know that in the time, 36 seconds, that it took to read a few paragraphs above (ok you fast readers, simmer down) a divorce is recorded? So in the 2.03 minutes it took American Pharaoh, 2015 Kentucky Derby Winner and Triple Crown winner, to cross the finish line at the Kentucky Derby approximately 4 divorces will cross the "I'm finished" line.[2]

Debby and I want to help stop couples getting to the "we're finished" line.

Do you want to beLIeVE?

We say YES or you wouldn't have this book in your hands.

Chapter 2
Let's Get Started: From Uncommon to Common

We don't come to you with all of the credentials, aka the initials behind our names that most of the writing/speaking guys and gals bring; however, what we do bring is a doctorate level of knowing how to be fake and people pleasing. You know that fake response when asked, "How are you guys doing?" And the response "I'm fine" comes flying out of your mouth as you dare not let anyone know that you and your marriage are a train wreck. So "masks" come out that have a pretty painted face that portrays the image you want the world to believe.

All of us have experienced this mask-wearing on both sides of the mask. Think of the times when walking through the worship barn of your choice, or when you're working, or at a social event and the small surface talk is flowing. Remember the questions about the weather, or of what's been going on in your world? And the responses -

"Oh nothing much,"

 "Same ol', same ol',"

"….life is really busy right now, how about you guys?"

Heads start noddin'

"Yep yep same over here…"

"Cool...cool…awesome"

I wondered early in my recovery why the church (worship barn) was the last place for most to reveal their need for prayer, the need to have folks come alongside and provide encouragement. Yes, the body of Christ can be and often is a bloody place to lay your heart out there. This is all the more reason for grace and how grace is what binds us together through the mess of life. Wouldn't it be nice for church to be a place where you can learn and see who can handle your heart with care? Therefore beLIeVING the words throughout the Book (Bible) where you are encouraged to pray with one another, encourage one another, and think of ways to motivate one another...OH yeah, and there is one in particular that Jesus was fond of. Love one another!

Debby and I understand and realize that our healing, our recovery will continue until we see Jesus face to face, releasing the battle of "we have to be fine" all the time mentality. Life is tough and grace is messy and pretending that it's not is bondage; it's hypocritical. When life is shared it provides these beautiful moments where someone can say "me too" and "Yeah let's pray with one another!"

Mask-Wearing

For me (Mike), wearing a mask started in my middle school years when at a friend's house (or really a guy who I wanted to be friends with because in my 13 year old mind he was part of the "popular' crowd, the "in crowd." Ever wonder why that crowd is deemed popular when they are the ones that are doing exactly what we don't want our kids to be doing? Anyway, you get where I'm coming from). His (Trey's) parents were gone and there were several people at his house and yes,

there were substances. Trey reached into a cooler that was jam-packed of full of ice and 8oz Miller Ponies.

Yep, they came in that size in 1977. As I reached out to grab the beer being offered to me, everything on the inside of my being was screaming, "NO! DON'T. THIS ISN'T YOU!" Yet the desire to fit in, the unwillingness to test the waters of "will they like me if I refuse the beer?" trumped the moment and I took my first drink of many that night. The next morning I lay motionless on the couch back at my house reeling from the effects of helping to empty out that cooler of Miller Ponies. My mama asked, "Michael, what is wrong with you?" My response, "Mama, I guess I ate too many donuts."

That was the moment the mask went on. The mask that says to a world with made up stories, that we want you to believe we really are fine, when deep down we are dying from shame, guilt, and embarrassment. We dare not let anyone see this. We pull our emotional bootstraps up, we put our big girl panties on, and we fake it. We lie to the very ones we are to trust the most. That self-applied mask stayed on tight and wore many colors throughout my high school, college, and corporate career and in the first 11 years of our marriage. The mask didn't start coming off until 2001 when the blue lights of a Knoxville sheriff pulled me over and booked me into their county jail for 24 hours for driving under the influence.

Debby: Free spirited, pleaser of a middle child, my desire to be loved and accepted by everyone I knew ultimately led me to put on a wardrobe full of masks. "Oh, you need me to be…?

Okay (hesitation), I'm good with that." California girl turned Southern Belle in the summer before my 7th grade year required the first mask to be put in place. I talk funny? (Note to self... change your accent.) I don't dress preppy enough? (Head to the nearest store for an Izod shirt and a pair of painter pants.) You won't love me unless I do what? (Okay, if that's what it takes.) Growing up with masks only makes the costume more elaborate as you get older because you have more to cover. So when you are 21 years old, madly in love with this curly headed, New York Yankee ball cap-wearing boy and the news comes that you're pregnant, my "good girl, this doesn't happen in our family" mentality mask had to be firmly put in place, and the most excruciating mistake we have ever made came knocking at our door. Mike and I had more in common than we realized, and when you live life not being your true self with others, especially with your spouse, a whole myriad of problems await.

Chapter 3
FOUNDation: Discovering Ourselves and Each Other

My little brown eyed bride of 26 years, Debby, walks in the kitchen and says "Hey, Mike let's paint the bathroom".… I hide my initial body language of CRAP and state, "Well ok, what color?" She informs me that she would like to paint the bathroom blue. Upon receiving that information I am down and away in a single bound to our local home improvement store to retrieve the royal blue of Middle Tennessee State University. Home of the Blue Raiders: True Blue, baby! Crash through the door singing, "Come see those blue raiders ride today," rollers in hand, smile of accomplishment on my skull, and notice that my bride is not as excited as I. What? I take a mental inventory. I was singing on key and my pitch was spot on. But the look, I've seen this posture before, yes I'm sure I've experienced this stance she is taking. As a matter of fact, it's The Look (body language is 55% of how we communicate[3]). What in the h___ is that? Along with the words - YIKES - (tone is 38%[3]) has kicked in on top as she is pointing at our (uh, my) purchase….the words were few, the impact received.

She then speaks with eyebrows raised….

"I said blue."

I respond, "Uh yeah" (now my head is starting to go to defensive tilt, eyebrows raised, raising cain) "This is blue. MTSU blue, the only blue there is baby, royal blue!"

Now you may know where I'm going…. the blue she has in her mind is a bit different than the blue in my mind and until she lets me know that her blue is robin's egg blue, we will continue to go back and forth saying the same words yet with different meanings.

Therefore, communication is knowing and understanding that the words you are using to convey, to connect, to exchange information have the same definition and meaning as the person you are communicating with.

Do your blues match? Maybe, just maybe, that's the start to your answer "how did we get here?"

The world states that the three biggies that break up marriages are sex, money and children.

We disagree. We believe it's how we are communicating through those areas and areas we are avoiding to chat through. Are you finding areas of life where through your silence you "think" you are on the same page, yet deep down for years you haven't really known where the other person is? And sometimes you're not even sure where you are.

Could it be that you are unwilling to honestly share where you are because of past consequences - both spoken and unspoken? Or early in the relationship you experienced the fury that comes with unhealthy conflict. You know, the emotions that flare to where veins fueled with venom are popping up all over your body and the battle is on.

Uncommon ground - how did you get here?

It's how you communicate through not only the big three we just mentioned, but also how you deliver and receive statements and comments from those you are conversing with, especially your spouse. What exactly does this word communicate mean? Depending on the dictionary you search you will find that this means to exchange or impart information to another.[4] It's a way for us to connect. If you're speaking in person you are not only hearing what the person is saying to you or AT you but you are also reading body language. Body language is a huge part of our exchange of information.

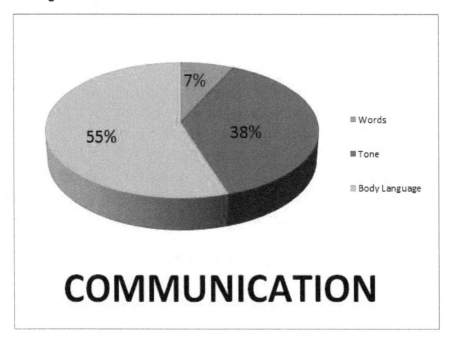

Isn't that remarkable? 93% of how we exchange information is non-verbal! Which means that whenever we are texting with each other, we are at a 93% deficit because we aren't able to hear tone or read body language. Encouragement: Do not have emotional or serious conversations over text.

DIGGIN' IN:

Take a look at the emotion chart below.

Most of us are familiar with the broad base of emotions that we see in the chart above. Take another look at what could be underneath by reviewing the next chart

List of Feelings

Happy	Sad	Angry	Other feelings
Calm	Ashamed	Annoyed	Afraid
Cheerful	Awful	Bugged	Anxious
Confident	Disappointed	Destructive	Bored
Content	Discouraged	Disgusted	Confused
Delighted	Gloomy	Frustrated	Curious
Excited	Hurt	Fuming	Embarrassed
Glad	Lonely	Furious	Jealous
Loved	Miserable	Grumpy	Moody
Proud	Sorry	Irritated	Responsible
Relaxed	Unhappy	Mad	Scared
Satisfied	Unloved	Mean	Shy
Silly	Withdrawn	Violent	Uncomfortable
Terrific			Worried
Thankful			
Tickled			

At times we aren't able to articulate the actual emotion that is roaring through and displaying itself through our body language. It's way ok to have these handy to refer to when you are chatting through life, especially the areas of life that stir up a multitude of emotions.

Or how about the moments when you hesitantly ask, "How are you doing?" or "You ok?" The reason for asking is that you can clearly see from the body language and facial distortion that your spouse is not in the most approachable frame of mind. Yet her reply is "oh I'm fine" as the arms cross and the shoulders start to turn away. The response of "I'm fine" along with the body language is not jiving together. Ah...now you know what we are talking about!

PAUSE and TIMEOUT

Now if you are flowing through this with your spouse, we do recommend that you both get a sheet of paper and something to write with so you can write your answers then share with one another. The purpose of doing this is to help you find your voice. When you live life with another person (your spouse), over the months and years you have discovered the land mines. Land mines are the explosions that occur from past relational wounds brought into the present. It's those touchy subjects in life where you say to yourself after setting off the land-mine, "I'll never bring that up again," and you start to stuff (hide, wear a mask) how you truly feel in a given situation. In the initial stuffing, the keeping our thoughts to ourselves doesn't seem to be a big deal; however, you can only bury so many landmines before they are deto-nated. As we just learned, you also learn how to read each other's eyes, body language, and tone in lightning speeds. The processing of the 93% (remember body language and tone) along with the words can alter how you really want to respond as you desire to avoid setting others off.

We have some friends who have a military background that would call the detonations - "C4 moments." It didn't take much for my limited knowledge to understand their meaning. These were close to nuclear events where battle lines had been drawn between the two, de-claring the other the enemy, or in other words, "you're not for me." "I thought you wanted the best for me, for us" ....the pressure of hiding (stuffing our real emotional state) will come on out, it's just when/where and how volatile.

Jot your response to the question below without your spouse seeing, then reveal your responses to each other simultaneously.

What is the emotion that best describes where you are right now.

The chart describing emotions help put a name to where we are doesn't it? How about we make a pact with each other here. From this point on you will no longer state "I'm fine" when you are not. You will not reply "I'm ok" if you're not. Detox from expecting your spouse to read your mind and start to trust each other for what and how you communicate with each other. Begin to make a habit of taking one another at their word. If you spouse says "I'm fine" but his/her body language is saying something different, practice saying "Okay, I'm going to take you at your word, but your body language is saying different."

Where are you?

When couples come to visit with Debby and me for a tune up or if their marriage is on the gurney heading into the ER, one of the first questions we pose to them to answer individually is "Is your spouse for you?" By FOR you we mean "Does your spouse desire the very best for you? Does your spouse support you?"

Remember, your spouse is not your enemy (and land mines are only buried for enemies). In the perceived effort to keep the peace, we are, in reality, empowering the true enemy (Satan) to separate us.

Take a moment to pray through this with your spouse. Ask God to reveal those areas that you have buried. Ask for wisdom to know why you have buried those land mines and how to disarm them.

Remember gang silence is the enemy's most effective weapon. It was silence in the garden where Adam and Eve did not communicate with each other before the crunch of the fruit. It is our silence with each other that creates an enormous chasm in our hearts. Silence creates wondering, and when we wonder enough then we will wander. We will wander to someone or something to ease the pain of the silence that creates the emotional disconnect in our marriages.

This question will determine your next steps

Are you ready to find the common ground of your hearts?

Good, let's keep moving.

 DIGGIN' IN:

Each person get a sheet of paper and pen or pencil. Remember the purpose is so you will answer with rigorous honesty.

Do you believe that your spouse is for you? By "FOR" you, we mean does your spouse wish the best for you? Does your spouse have your best interest in mind? Does your spouse support you? We begin our journey by determining what you believe deep down: is your spouse FOR you?

Ok, ready? Write your answer (no cheating, don't look at the responses until time).

Have you answered yes or no? (No long explanations here, gang...simply respond yes or no).

OK ready to show each other?

ONE.......TWO.....THREE....WAIT WAIT...

Are you wondering what your spouse wrote? If so. That's called jumping in the other person's hoop (to be discussed later), so let's not wonder (or wander).

Now let's go ONE.....TWO....THREE....turn 'em over and share!

Did your responses match what you thought?

Example: Some couples will answer on their sheet NO
No in that they do not believe their spouse wants or desires the best for them, only to find that their spouse has answered yes. Yes they do want the best for them.

What did you discover?

Most of the time - the answers are yes, both people realize that they are for each other, meaning that deep down they believe the person they said, "I do and I will" with does love them and desires the best for them.

What if one of you answered no? Now if one of you answers no - meaning no, you don't believe your spouse desires the best for you, the trust in the relationship is broken. The spouse who does not believe the other desires the best for them will not trust the motive of whatever comes out of the mouth of the other. Your guard is up and in deflect/protect mode. This is the genesis, the launching point that creates the initial communication snafus.

For example, think about those moments on car lots, in cellular phone stores, and kiosks in malls, when the salesperson is rolling information at you 5000 miles an hour and underneath you are thinking, "I don't trust this person as far as I can throw them." This heart-set places you in protect mode, which has you internally questioning any and every thing that is being fired at you. When you don't believe that your spouse is for you, the words coming from your spouse will seem to be zooming at you at the same warp speed and the words are deflecting off of you like bullets on rocks in a John Wayne movie. You are not allowing anything to penetrate the bridge you have rolled up around your heart. You are in lock-down mode.

If one of the responses is no, we recommend you find a local therapist, life coach, or someone you trust that can help you walk through when and where you started to believe your spouse wasn't and isn't for you. You will want to discover if you are feeding the truth or a lie. Where did you start to not trust the motive of the other person in this relationship? What this will do is help you realize when and where one or both either gave up or started hiding within the relationship.

For those that did have a "no" in the response, PLEASE follow through and find someone to help you walk through the next steps. Our information is provided at the end of this book if you want to contact us. We can help you find someone in your area that can help you take the steps needed to start on the foundation of knowing that even through the conflict that deep down you do desire the best for each other. In some cases, through infidelity, financial stress, job loss, relocation, addiction, co-addicts, the trust we once had for another has been shattered. You may want someone to walk you through some individual counseling before you start working on the marriage. Final thought on this before we move on: even if you read through these pages on your own, it will help you identify where you started to move away from your spouse emotionally. When we heal individually through Christ our marriages start to heal.

We will proceed on the premise that both of you said, "YES, we are for one another" and that you both believe the yes.

Moving from unCommon to Common

One of the first eye-opening discoveries in walking back to common ground for a marriage is when you believe that your spouse is not for you, then find out that your spouse wrote yes. The work now is to discover why you thought they were not for you. This will be revealed when we teach you how to chat with each other.

The next question is "**Where are you spiritually?**" Now you might be thinking, "Uh what does this have to do with where we are in our relationship?" Our answer is EVERY-THING! Most of you were probably married by a pastor, reverend, or minister. You stated promises to one another with words like "till death do us part" or "for better or for worse." Maybe you were some of the adventurous ones who wrote some of your vows. The words you scripted and repeated for one another flowed from a depth of your heart you didn't realize you had. Words like "forever," "love like no one else," "you are my everything…" Most of you even had words from the man officiating. He talked about Christ and how you are to submit to one another out of reverence for Christ (Ephesians 5:21). But now when your spouse opens his/her mouth, feelings that were once full of love are now full of venom, bitterness, resentment, hurt, and sadness. Doesn't this leave us at least considering "how do we submit to one another out of reverence for Christ?"

The reason for the question is to help you both discover who Christ is for you individually and in your marriage.

Debby and I were not always on common ground in our faith. She was head over heels in love with Jesus and I loved myself or thought I did. As we walked through the day to day there was no way for me to submit to her out of reverence for Christ, because I didn't know Him. She did, and only by the power of the Holy Spirit within her could she carry on with me in the condition I was living. For me (men) to love Debby (our wives) as Christ loved the church,

I had to know who Jesus was (and still is!) and why he loved the church (us).

 # DIGGIN' IN:

Write your answers, then reveal to each other:

Where are you spiritually? _____

Write your response then share with each other.

Did you know or struggle with how to answer the question?

The response that we receive most of the time when we ask this question is "I/we go to such and such church"…our reply "That's a great worship barn (our term for bricks and mortar facilities that are called churches) however that's not what we asked."

We ask again "Where are you spiritually?"

Now that you know we are looking for something a bit deeper let's have another go at it.

Where are you spiritually? _____

Maybe this will help:

Was there a day you said "YES!" to Jesus?

Why did you say yes? Your response could have been:
"I wanted to ask Jesus into my heart"
"I wanted to be saved"
"I didn't want to go to hell"
"My mom or dad said it was time"
"My sister/friend did so I did too"

"I felt pressured"

_____ (Other)

Does this have you thinking a bit? Good! Remember, you want and desire to discover where you are and how you enabled each other to get to this point. By placing Christ in the center of our individual lives He automatically becomes the center - the power center - for the marriage.

Let us ask the question another way;

How is your faith, your yes to Christ helping you today?

Share the reason you said "YES!" to Jesus with your spouse. Answer on our sheet of paper then share (don't rush through this one).

Chapter 4
Our Helper: HIM Within
(The Power Center of Your Marriage)

Welcome back! Why is discovering where you are with Jesus important? Today when you are sitting with someone to whom you said, "I do and I will," but now you are at the point of "I'm out" and "I won't…" You have to understand the importance of seeking Christ in your marriage. You are learning and understanding how HE can help us in seeking common ground in our differences.

Knowing why we are married and should stay married is crucial. The key question is this: Will we approach marriage from a God-centered view or a self-centered view? In a self-centered view, we will maintain our marriage as long as our earthly comforts, desires, and expectations are met. In a God-centered view, we preserve our marriage because it brings glory to God and points a sinful world to a reconciling Creator.
Gary Thomas, author of Sacred Marriage

Read John 14:16-17

And I will ask the Father, and he will give you another Advocate, who will never leave you. He is the Holy Spirit, who leads into all truth. The world cannot receive him, because it isn't looking for him and doesn't recognize him. But you know him, because he lives with you now and later will be in you.

Now answer the above question: Why is discovering where you are with Jesus important?

 DIGGIN' IN:

Why did Jesus tell us this before he placed himself on the cross? Go ahead and provide answers and see where you both are.

When do I allow the Holy Spirit of Christ to help me?

Maybe the following questions will help you see where we spend our hours

How many hours at work?

How many hours sleeping?

How many hours at your place of worship?

There are 168 hours in a week (24 hour days times 7 days). Take a look at the table and pie chart below that help provide a visual of where our time is spent during the 168 hours.

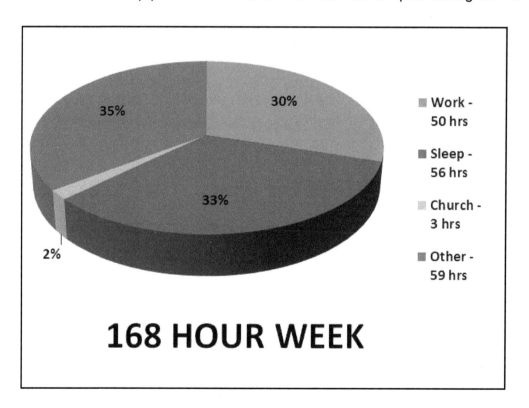

Let's put this in perspective. 8 hours at work, then 8 hours of sleep gives us 16 hours of the 24 hour day. That's 67% of our time spent at home and at work (excluding weekends).

Where do we have the biggest opportunity to show the world our faith? Exactly! In our homes, at work, in our schools, in the community which all involve how we communicate in relationships including our marriages. It's how we show a world how to have healthy, transparent, and authentic conversations that strengthen and not tear down.

Recall the verse you read earlier. Why does Jesus say (paraphrase) Look gang I'm going to send a helper, someone that will help lead you, someone that will bring comfort, someone that will counsel you, heck someone who is for you...ahhhh the words we long to hear. He says, "I'm for you, I want the best for you." That's God's desire for us. Could it be that Jesus knew the trials and sorrows we would experience in our homes, at work, in our marriages, and in our relationships and that we would need HIS help to travel through?

The answer is a resounding YES!

So be truly glad. There is wonderful joy ahead, even though you have to endure many trials for a little while. These trials will show that your faith is genuine. It is being tested as fire tests and purifies gold--though your faith is far more precious than mere gold. So when your faith remains strong through many trials, it will bring you much praise and glory and honor on the day when Jesus Christ is revealed to the whole world.
1Peter 1:6-7
I have told you all this so that you may have peace in me. Here on earth you will have many trials and sorrows. But take heart, because I have overcome the world."
John 16:33

 DIGGIN' IN:

If Jesus has overcome the world, and when we said yes to HIM he resides within us, to help guide and direct our lives.

When and where do I ever acknowledge that I need help?

And the bigger question is how... how do you allow the HIM within (Holy Spirit) to help you through your daily lives that will flow to and through ALL of your relationships including your marriage to find common ground?

List your answers then share with one another.

What did you find out about yourself?

What did you find out about your spouse?

If you struggled to answer any of the questions, no worries at all gang as there are ton of "me too's" out here with us. Debby and I too had to learn the significance and importance of what we are asking you now. Only a few have been able to share how the holy Spirit guides their lives. HIM within is our battle cry when referring to the indwelling of the Holy Spirit.

QUICK thought; If this is an area where you would like to have someone come along side, pray with each other in seeking who are the people in your lives that your trust to teach.

When you understand the significance of your faith then you as a couple can start to beLIeVE (live) out the words Paul stated in Ephesians 5 where he tells us to submit to one another out of reverence for Christ...in order for this to happen we have to know who Chris is and who He is within us.

How to beLIeVE HIM within? (time to be honest and vulnerable)
How do you allow the Christ living within us (Holy Spirit) to lead us? I mean you hear all of these words, clichés in the barns all of the time, yet not many are teaching (discipling) how to do so. Not many are letting others know in the barn they hang out in for the .004% of the week that they are weak and weary (that's for another eBook).

How many of your friends know if your marriage is struggling?

If no one, why?

Remember gang the place and people we worship with each week is our family. It can be a place where we show the world that no matter what life brings we are united and strengthened through our pain and celebration.

Find some like hearted folks who know how to care for your heart and you theirs. Look what you will be living out. so the prayers offered on your behalf will help reveal the Way of Christ in your heart then flow to others in your home, at work, at school, and in the community in how you beLIeVE (James 5, Galatians 6:23).

TIMEOUT

Go get ya something to drink and take a deep breath! You're doing great so far. Let's help you with applying the how to in the verses you just read.

Welcome back
Guys a quick reminder for you to go the pace that is beneficial for both. If either one is just plowing through to "get er done". Hoping that after you finish this will just vanish. Please put it down for a day or 2, high five the progress made and determine a time to take the next steps.

Let's summarize what you have discovered about each other:

- You have discovered that you are for each other, which means that you both want and desire the best for each other.
- You have discovered that sometimes you are saying similar words yet with different meaning. Your understanding, your knowing is off just a bit (your blues don't quite match).
- Through beLIeVING in the death, burial, and resurrection of Jesus Christ you are equipped with the Mighty Counselor, the Helper (Holy Spirit) to keep you united and guide you daily.
- You are learning to be able to communicate at a deeper and more meaningful level.

Chapter 5
PRIORITIES: HE'S IN EVERYTHING

Don't you realize that your body is the temple of the Holy Spirit, who lives in you and was given to you by God? You do not belong to yourself...
1 Corinthians 6:19

...and this hope will not lead to disappointment. For we know how dearly God loves us, because he has given us the Holy Spirit to fill our hearts with his love.
Romans 5:5

Now you have learned, discovered, or have been reminded that Jesus' favorite dwelling place is within us. This means you have resurrection power living inside you! (HIM within).

Isn't that amazing! Come on, read that again. You have resurrection, tomb blasting, grace loving, and mercy - giving POWER within you....YES YES YES! HIM WITHIN!

When God entered our marriage in 2001 (remember we said "I do" to each other in '89 so 12 years later) we realized one week while on vacation in one of our favorite places, the white sandy beaches of Destin, that God can't be a line item in our lives....

He is in everything!

The example that hit home was when we were cleaning up from the beach one day and we were picking up the buckets from the day of play. You know the buckets that you procure from the grocery store or the nearest souvenir shop. The multi-color buckets that come nested in each other with the little plastic shovel, packaged in that plastic mesh...Well to us, God is the biggest bucket where all of the other buckets (priorities) nest into ONE.

If Jesus is holding all creation together, and

if everything was made through Him and for Him, including our marriages, you can let go and let God. Meaning that by beLIeVING and through seeking help from HIM within you are able to navigate through any circumstance or situation where your "blues aren't matching."

Paul reminds us in his letter to the saints in Colosse that:

Christ is the visible image of the invisible God. He existed before anything was created and is supreme over all creation, for through him God created everything in the heavenly realms and on earth. He made the things we can see and the things we can't see--such as thrones, kingdoms, rulers, and authorities in the unseen world. Everything was created through him and for him. He existed before anything else, and he holds all creation together.
Colossians 1:15-17

 DIGGIN' IN:

You will need more paper for this one. Take yourself back to the days when you first met and started hanging out with each other. If married, think of the engagement time frame up to marriage…it's that time when you were both in WOW mode with each other. It's that time of your relationship when your phone rang and your spouse's name came flashing across the screen. Man o man you couldn't answer the call fast enough could you? Always anticipating the joy of just hearing each other's voice.

Have that time frame in your mind?

What we want you to do now is to list the priorities you believe your spouse was living out before he/she was your spouse. We are looking at the dating, engagement, and the early years in your marriage. When you list the priorities place yourself in the list.

Take a look at ours as an example:

Here is my list (Mike) that reflects what I thought Debby's priorities were when we first started hanging out (1987) and I'm placing myself in the list:

- Finishing school (getting a "real" job)
- Spending time with each other (so this would include me)
- Family
- Hanging out with her buddies

Debby's list for Mike's priorities looked like this:
- Softball
- Herself
- When the next party was going to be
- Friends

The lists reveal that our lives demonstrated our desire to have each other as a priority. In this season we were on common ground.

YOUR TURN

Write the top 5 priorities of your spouse when you first started hanging out and place yourself on the list.

1.
2.
3.
4.
5.

(Remember, don't let the other see)

Make sure you're on the list somewhere!

Now share your list with your spouse.
Were you higher on the list than you thought? Or lower?

Most couples will have the each other listed in the top 2 of the list.

Take time here to recall some of the times you spent together before life crept in. I bet you are smiling at some of those memories, aren't you?

You may recall that the early years have fewer distractions, or you hadn't allowed anyone or anything to come in between your oneness, then life starts to invade. The reasons are many and varied.

WHERE DID OUR ROADS SEPARATE?

Now in just a bit we want you to perform the same exercise that you just completed but this time you will list the priorities of each other as you experience today. Debby and I will give you a glimpse of how and where the road started to split for us.

Mike:

Jesus didn't penetrate my world until 2001. I was climbing the corporate ladder; full speed ahead in the ole rat race, gonna be the one to win the race or reach the top. Not realizing at the time there is no winner or top. Corporate America is a thirsty animal and being a piece of the machine left me thirsty yet in a different way...I was starting to have conversations with myself. The conversations would revolve around the fact that deep down I realized I had an identity problem. On the outside confidence was flowing, yet on the inside insecurities were roaring. This manifested in me seeking the career and alcohol to compensate or medicate the insecurities of unbelief. When you don't know who and/or whose you are, you will grab at the very things of the world to try and help you feel better. Paul told the Corinthians about this in his letter. Check this out.

We grow weary in our present bodies, and we long to put on our heavenly bodies like new clothing. For we will put on heavenly bodies; we will not be spirits without bodies. While we live in these earthly bodies, we groan and sigh, but it's not that we want to die and get rid of these bodies that clothe us. Rather, we want to put on our new bodies so that these dying bodies will be swallowed up by life. God himself has prepared us for this, and as a guarantee he has given us his Holy Spirit.
2 Corinthians 5:2-5

This makes SOOO much sense to me. Remember the question earlier - how is your faith helping you today? Here is an example:

Remember I stated that my career and booze was a by-product of the identity crisis I had earlier. It's like Paul is stating in the letter I was groaning, just wasn't content, satisfied, therefore I reached for the "things" of the world and for most men it's work. Listen to a conversation where men are first meeting and within the first 3 questions they will ask the other where they work. It's a way to size each other up. It's a false feeding thus leaving you empty each night you go home from the day because you are showing this false self to the world … Henry Cloud has a great way of sharing this in his book Changes that Heal: How to Understand Your Past to have a Healthier Future.

When the real self comes into relationship with God and others, an incredible dynamic is set into motion: we grow as God created us to grow.

Problems occur when the real self, the one God created, is hiding from God and others. If the true self is in hiding, the false self takes over. The false self is the self that is conformed to this world (Rom. 12:2). The false self is the self we present to others, the false front, if you will, that we put up for others to see.

January 2001: The blue lights of a Knoxville sheriff pulled over the false self as I was driving down the road with my lights off both literally and figuratively. The words that had worked in the past to get me off the hook from officers were not setting in with this guy. The field sobriety test confirmed what he and I both knew. My life was out of control. The false self had to die.

The "you get one phone call" was not made to my bride. The call was made to those who were with me so they could call the people who could get me out of this trouble, who could save me from anyone ever having to know. Could someone please just come bury this?

I sat for 24 hours in a holding tank in an orange white striped jumpsuit. Sitting in regret, embarrassment, shame, and self-condemnation, with the 'what if's' flying all around. I admitted to myself what I had not been willing to admit. Oh sure, I knew deep down in the depths of my being I was a wreck, but the outside was "functioning" right? NO. This was different. I had reached the bottom.

The guys were coming and I didn't know what to do.

Before I walked out of that cell I admitted I was a functional alcoholic and I needed help. There in that cell I performed the first step of admitting I was powerless and my life was out of control. Looking back, it's not a far jump for me to realize that step 2 was being poured in as well. It's the step in AA after admitting our powerlessness where one begins to acknowledge a higher power had to step in to takeover because me being my own god was not getting it done in my life and in my marriage.

That day was the start of the change of my power center.

The guys arrived and assured me that no one would ever have to know, not even my bride. Years before, even hours before, I would have jumped at that opportunity to keep the false self going. Not today. I had to make a change. I listened and thanked them and let them know that I was tired of running. Not sure why I was running or who I was, but I was tired.

On my way home, I stopped in Crossville, TN to call Debby and let her know that I needed to chat with her. I didn't provide any specifics. Upon my arrival, the kiddos were not home, and I proceeded to share with my bride what happened hours earlier. As I finished, I was not sure what I was going to hear. I braced myself for anything, knowing I deserved whatever was about to come AT me. I hear these words flow from underneath the brown eyes filled with tears. "I guess some things will change" and for the very first time in my life I experienced grace. There was no "I told you so"…no anger…no verbally beating me up; she knew I was doing a pretty good job of that myself.

She was speaking from HIM within - her power center. And our lives did start to change.

In this season, my list for Debby would have been:
1. God (remember this is prior to my 2001 realization that HE is in all)
2. Kids
3. Choir (church)
4. Me
5. Buddies

See how i moved from top 2 to 4? Slow fade gang…life will creap in when we empower it to do so.

Debby: In 1998 I was the wife of a man whose identity came through who he was at work and the fun-loving, life of the party he was at play. As a momma of two, the wide-open, weekend life left me empty. I continually said to myself, "There's got to be more to this life than this." I had this new friend who oozed Jesus wherever she was. She didn't just talk Christianese on Sundays, she allowed Him to live His life through her every other day of the week. She had hope outside her own circumstances. I desperately wanted what she had. So I began to live out the verse that says, "Seek me and you will find me, when you seek me with all your heart" (Jeremiah 29:13). I began to ask Jesus to change my desires for Him and He did. I immersed myself in every new Bible study; I began journaling daily and reading God's word for guidance in my every day. I said "yes" to everything that church had to offer (some good, but looking back, not all were God's best yes for me). Then it happened...*Breaking Free* by Beth Moore.

Remember the Debby with the closet full of masks? Well, I had one particular mask that I wore for 10 years. In choosing my way instead of God's way, and the unquenchable need to be loved, accepted, and pleasing in every aspect of my life, when a 21 year old girl and a 23 year old boy find themselves pregnant and not married, I had only one choice in order to keep the mask and my image: abortion. Because I had no idea who I was, when I made that dreaded phone call to Mike to tell him I was pregnant, and he said, "What do you want to do?" I knew another layer of the mask had to be put in place. I didn't realize the pressure that settled in my spirit that said, "This decision is yours to make." From that moment on, I took full responsibility for the shame, because after all, I made the decision and it was my body. To say I wasn't initially relieved would be a lie, but the cloak of secret shame was a garment I wore in silence for 10 years, until the dam broke wide open in 1998 and I blurted my secret out to room full of unsuspecting women and received nothing but grace. True freedom in Christ started that day for me, and I have never been the same. Freedom has been a process, like the peeling back of an onion. I had many lies to dispel, only to be replaced with new firm truths. In addition to Breaking Free, God used the study Surrendering the Secret to totally unlock me.

Our son's name is Tanner. He would have been born January 1989. Through this freedom, my biggest nightmare has been transformed into the child of my dreams. I will see him one day. I am sure of it. I have a flower that returns every summer in his honor. It's the Black-eyed Susan, but forever to me they will be my Tanner flowers.

Mike and I were not on the same page spiritually. As he said, he checked the church box every week, but probably to keep peace with me. I was crazy in love with this new Jesus I discovered. Not this Judge that would allow me to barely sneak in the doors of heaven, but this amazing God that was crazy in love with me, despite my choices!

This is what I believe Mike's priorities were in this season:
- Work/climbing the corporate ladder
- Alcohol
- Hobbies
- Providing for our family
- Me

Wow wow wow see this gang? Top two down to five…both of us have allowed life to take over.

This may be an example of where you are today. Your lives that once were on common ground, you were on the same page, you were on the same road…there were NO fence posts between you. Life has now found you moving down each other's list of priorities: kids, jobs, hobbies have come in between.

If this is where you both find yourselves, as crazy as this sounds you can celebrate this moment, as you are on common ground in discovering that you have allowed life to come before your oneness. In essence you are enablers. You might be struggling with this label, but when you write your list ask yourself:

Who empowered this decision?

Yep, you make decisions that allow your spouse to fall down the list in your life.

Ok now you can give each other high five...easy now...make sure we hit the palms ha-haha...

 DIGGIN' IN: (let's see where you are)

Write your list of how you see your spouse's priorities today and place yourself in that list.
1.
2.
3.
4.
5.

(Remember, no looking. This is where you will remind yourself constantly we are for each other.)

Take this slow gang, and start to unpack where you believe the fence posts started to grow. Recall that your lives were on common ground, you were tracking together, on the same wave length, no one hiding, there were no fence posts between you. Yet now both are looking up over new jobs, hobbies, the kids, the you name it's in life that we have allowed to come in between or receive higher priority than each other.

As crazy as this sounds, celebrate this moment. It just may be the first time you have been honest and vulnerable with each other since you first started chasing each other. Celebrate that right now you are on common ground in realizing both have enabled life to take over.

Debby and I share with folks that, as you start to move each other back up the list, you have to take the stance that NOTHING can or will come in between your oneness even if you birthed 'em (kids, careers, hobbies, etc.). YOU give birth to activity that separates you...you are HIMpowered to place each other as priorities in your lives.

Chapter 6
FORGIVENESS

Forgiveness is just letting go of the offense (you're not saying it was ok, but what you are saying is that you're no longer holding the person hostage from the pain that was inflicted). You are saying, "I choose to allow the blood of Christ (the empty tomb) to cover you as I am covered". You are saying, "I'm no longer going to allow 'this' to hinder our relationship."

That's what God said, that He would no longer allow sin to hinder the relationship He desires with us

Take a peek:

So Christ has now become the High Priest over all the good things that have come. He has entered that greater, more perfect Tabernacle in heaven, which was not made by human hands and is not part of this created world. With his own blood--not the blood of goats and calves--he entered the Most Holy Place once for all time and secured our redemption forever.
Hebrews 9:11-12
...so also Christ died once for all time as a sacrifice to take away the sins of many people. He will come again, not to deal with our sins, but to bring salvation to all who are eagerly waiting for him.
Hebrews 9:28
For God's will was for us to be made holy by the sacrifice of the body of Jesus Christ, once for all time.
Hebrews 10:10
Christ suffered for our sins once for all time. He never sinned, but he died for sinners to bring you safely home to God. He suffered physical death, but he was raised to life in the Spirit.
1 Peter 3:18

I just love the 'once for all time' verses. Let that sink in: especially take another peek where Peter reminds us that Christ was raised to life in the Spirit. It's the same resurrection, Holy Spirit power that resides in you and me when we said yes to Jesus (faith, believe). The

Holy Spirit hasn't jumped out of you because of where or what you have done. God has purchased us through Christ.

He is so rich in kindness and grace that he purchased our freedom with the blood of his Son and forgave our sins…The Spirit is God's guarantee that he will give us the inheritance he promised and that he has purchased us to be his own people. He did this so we would praise and glorify him.
Ephesians 1:7, 14
That through Christ we are holy and blameless, nothing will be held against us. Yet now he has reconciled you to himself through the death of Christ in his physical body. As a result, he has brought you into his own presence, and you are holy and blameless as you stand before him without a single fault.
Colossians 1:22

As you continue to flow through your list, is there an area in your marriage that needs the extended heart of grace and forgiveness in order to move forward?

What you are saying and displaying is that through the power of Christ within us (Holy Spirit) you no longer will allow anyone or anything to hinder your relationship with each other.

Example from Debby
I (Debby) knew that God was doing something in my own heart as it pertained to forgiveness when He began to change my bitter mind and nagging words into a prayer of transformation for our lives and our marriage. A constant prayer began to take over that said, "Lord, do whatever You have to do to make Mike come to the end of himself. Please protect him and help him not to hurt himself or physically hurt someone else." Only a few months later, he sat on the couch and shared with me that he was arrested for DUI. I know that God had been preparing and softening my heart to see my broken man the way He did and allowed me to release him (forgive him) from the consequences that had stolen so much from our marriage.

Forgiveness is a verb for us and has action. We are in a constant state of release of one another as we live this messy life of grace. It's work. It's hard. But the fruit that it has lavished on our marriage is immeasurable.

If so, do you know how to forgive?

If not, please find someone that can help you walk through how…

 # DIGGIN' IN:

Are there any areas in your marriage you believe are unresolved, or haven't been reconciled? Is there doubt lingering within or an area that needs forgiveness once and for all time?

Disclaimer: please please please don't rush through this, when in doubt ask people you trust to guide you through forgiveness. It's huge in order for healing to occur and maintain the foundation of knowing that you are for each other

Here are some examples:
- Have you forgiven yourself?
- Do you believe your spouse has forgiven you?
- Do you love yourself?
- Do you beLIeVE you are worthy to be loved?
- Have you forgiven each other?

If you have answered no to any of the questions listed above, the ability to move forward is hampered and difficult. Remember the first question and the statement to constantly remind ourselves is: "Is your spouse for you? Do you believe your spouse desires the best for you?" If a "no" response is attached to any of the above, you will not trust the motive of your spouse which in turn means you don't believe they are for you.

Also:

If you don't beLIeVE you are worthy to be loved, then you reject yourself before others have a chance. You won't allow yourself to drink in the love others are offering, starting with your spouse (remember is he/she for me?)

You may say that you forgive others, yet if you are holding onto unforgiveness for yourself then it does spill out to rejecting others.

Remember God through Christ forgives in order for nothing to hinder our relationships. It's a great model to follow.

You must love yourself, you must know and beLIeVE that you are who God says you are through your yes to Jesus.

Chapter 7
STAY IN YOUR HOOP

Now that you have this discovery, this foundation of grace, what's next?

You start to talk **WITH** each other instead of **AT** each other, which will help you start moving each other back up the list. It's submitting to one another out of reverence for Christ.

How to chat (communicate) with each other vs "at" each other:

Did you ever hula hoop growing up? Man I never could get the knack for it. I would do that self-spin. You know the one where you rotate the hoop all the way to one side and ZING it across to the other side, attempting to help the hoop spin around your torso, only to have it fall effortlessly to the ground as your mind is wanting your hips to keep it going, yet the body just isn't able to respond. My bride on the other hand is a spinning machine. You know the ones that look like they aren't even moving and the hoop is rotating around their hips at speeds that leave you in awe.

Well picture that you are standing in that hoop or to illustrate, bring your hands out in front of you and then form a circle by stretching your arms to form circle with fingers touching in front of you.

Kinda like this guy:

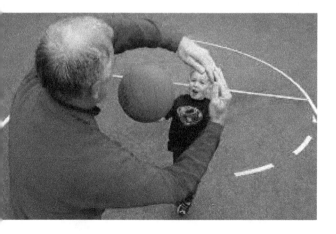

What can you control outside of the circle? YEP, nothing! Oh, we try mind you. We attempt to control a whole lotta "things" outside that circle including our spouses or those we have deep relationships with.

Picture that you are holding the hoop out and when someone asks you a question, the microcomputers in your brain start to manipulate possible results in how you should respond, based on how the person you are communicating with will react to our response. When you think you know how the other person will react, which is projecting, and you change/alter/package what you say, that's you jumping in the other person's hoop. It's a form of co-dependency when you alter your answer in order to make the other person feel better about you and/or themselves.

Quick reminder here...if the person I'm with is FOR me, then why would I not state the truth in all of my responses?

 DIGGIN' IN:

Here are some that debby and i experience and see with others
- Afraid of conflict
- Keeping the peace
- Avoid confrontation
- Bringing past hurtful response into this conversation

Let's list some of the reasons why you jump in others' hoops:

1.

2.

3.

4.

5.

Share your responses.

Yes or no with conflict

Hey who loves conflict?

Exactly most of us avoid this area at all costs, yet the cost is to much when our marriage is concerned. Break the silence and take a look.

All of our relationships should have healthy conflict.... key word being healthy. If there is not healthy conflict in your relationships then someone in the relationship is lying and/or hiding. Since all you have control over is what is in your hoop then all you can do is know that you are not lying and/or hiding.

Healthy conflict is when you communicate how you are processing and receiving the information in perceived and real disagreements. You are able to state your conflict in the moment you disagree, and you may end up agreeing to disagree; however, you are reminding each other that you are for each other, that nothing will separate you, and you are allowing each other to have freedom in thoughts and/or opinions.

DIGGIN' IN:

Are there any areas/topics in your marriage where you now realize you have been altering your response due to thinking and projecting how your spouse will react?

Yes or No_____

If Yes, what? _____

Why? _____

Write your response, then share.

Pray pray pray! Now is not the time to start hiding. Secrets kill! It's a different type of cancer that withers away at the interior of your being, starting with your heart. The reasons why you started to hide are many. What were your reasons earlier? Are you still enabling those?

Experience the freedom Christ talks about and discover that the way to rebuild trust, to help each other move up the list is to share openly while releasing expectations of responses.

Allow the HIM within to help you through what and where you have not been willing to travel.

Remember, since your discovery of where you are in each other's lives, you are setting your sights on placing each other in the proper place within your lives. This means you have determined that you will no longer hide in your relationships, that you will be truthful in all statements with yourself and each other. You want to continually remind each other that you want and desire the very best for the other person.

Let's say, for example, that you sidestep some topics within your daily conversations by staying silent – in other words, you "stuff" it. The reason behind this is that you are avoiding anger-- you know this area has caused abusive talk with each other. Your thought is "If I can stay silent maybe it will get better..." Silence says that's it ok to talk to and treat me in a man- ner that is unhealthy.

Or you are the one who is finally realizing you are being abusive but you're not quite sure.

Here is a question for you:

Would you allow another man/woman to come in and speak with your spouse in the same manner as you do/are?

Do you know how many have said yes?   Zilch, no one, nada.

If you wouldn't allow anyone else to speak to your spouse in the manner that you are, then why are you? This may be a time to go back to the section on forgiveness and walk this out with each other before proceeding.

Chapter 8
Healthy Conflict

Rules of Engagement

As you begin to discuss the areas where you have been altering, hiding, and/or avoiding in your relationship, it's very possible and most likely the hair on the back of your necks just might rise up, meaning anger/frustration will rise up. You will know you are in this heart set when the ol' heart rate starts to quicken, palms start to sweat, the pulse is quickening, and you are starting to get defensive. Your voice is just about to rise. Veins in the neck and noggin are beginning to bulge...

These are examples of our emotional dashboard flashing. As soon as you feel the first twinge of being defensive, call a timeout. Picture yourself driving to your favorite vacation spot and while in route the yellow lights start to flash reflecting your water temperature is rising. We notice the light, we know that we must pay attention to the light or the yellow light will turn to red, and yet a lot of times we ignore it, or we avoid it by placing a post it note over it.

That is what happens if we ignore our Emotional Dashboard. These are perfect examples of altering, hiding, and/or avoiding. If we don't call that timeout and, instead, just move on as if nothing is warning us within, it's a different form of post it note.

Here are some examples of Emotional Dashboard flashing post it notes:
"I'm fine..."
"Nothing, nothing is wrong..."
"He/she should know what's wrong so I'm not saying..."
Walking away...emotionally disengaging...
Telling yourself it doesn't matter...
Shutting down in fear of confrontation
Running/isolating

If we avoid these by placing our emotional post it notes over them and pretend, just like the water temperature gauge that is left unattended, the heat will begin to be too much and explosions will occur.

Do you understand, yet you're still fearful? Now you will understand the "why" behind saying "YES!" to Jesus. The Holy Spirit is the source of strength to carry us through the "I don't want to"...yet you have to...

The fur is up...The emotions within are starting to RISE. You call the timeout and:

Stop... drop and Pray ...

Recall the instructions we received as children, that if we ever had fire jump on us, we were to stop drop and roll

This is a different fire and we are saying stop drop and pray

When the emotional dashboard is flashing, we are wanting to flee or avoid that is the enemy trying to get in between what God joined together...Satan separates. The enemy knows that silence in the relationship can disrupt... Just ask Adam and Eve.

Bring the authority of the one who has rendered the enemy defeated.

STOP...DROP...and PRAY with and over each other in this moment...the enemy has to flee at the sound of Jesus' name.

So humble yourselves before God. Resist the devil, and he will flee from you.
James 4:7

The HIM within WINS....the stopping allows us to get the heart rates down, take a deep breath, and humble ourselves, which in Southern slang means to "get off your high horse" and let's pray this out with each other.

Remind each other that you are for one another. Slay the lie that you are each other's ene-my.

Remind yourself as you stop that your spouse is not the enemy. YES you certainly "feel like" he or she is your enemy at that moment, but he or she is not. The enemy, THE enemy is Satan--and remember what you just learned. At the sound of Jesus' name the enemy has to flee, and ask God to shine His Light of Truth into any darkness that may be in between you and your spouse.

There are times when my little brown eyed bride and I will have our fur flying and we call a timeout to stop, drop, and pray. Yet we have to grind through the mental/fleshy feeling within us that is saying "I don't want to pray." We create connection with each other by holding hands, and then pray over and with each other that in the name of Jesus Christ for HIM to shed light in this moment of darkness. Remind each other in the prayer that you are for one another...the HIM WITHIN WINS!

After you pray, give yourself some time to ask this question:

"What and or who was I defending and why?"

Have a designated agreed upon time to come back and continue the discussion. Ask each other how much time is needed. Depending on the area selected you may need more time than with the other areas in your lives that you have discovered that are coming in between you. Always, always, always, always, always come back to finish the discussion to find your common ground.

When you come back, remind each other that you are for each other. Are you starting to get the message? You must remind one another that you desire the best for each other. That your motive is not to harm.

Begin the conversation with what you learned about yourself in the discussion. Share what you were defending and then ask yourself why. Was your defense or your thought based on truth? Continue to move through the conversation seeking common ground. Continue to write out answers then reveal to each other. This helps you learn to trust your voice and not default to the old way of avoiding, by jumping in your spouse's hoop or giving in when dashboards begin to flash.

You will realize that that your mind is giving energy to areas in your marriage you just know is a hot button and your spouse isn't giving it a moment of thought. Those are fun EUREKA moments.

Summary of Healthy Conflict Flow

Healthy conflict is when we are able to communicate differences with one another and not "have to agree" to just keep peace.

- We are not altering our thoughts in order to make the other person feel better about us.
- Nor are we altering our viewpoint in order for the other person to be ok with us.
- We are staying in our hoop (see above for reminder if you're saying to yourself "stay in my what?")
- When the emotional dashboard flashes, we are not going to cover it up.
- We call time out STOP, DROP, PRAY and flow HIMpowered through the conversation.
- We are finding the common ground that is best for both of us.
- We are finding the common ground that is best for both (repeat on purpose).

Disclaimer: DO NOT...we repeat DO NOT have these conversations in your bedroom. That is to be your palace, so if your bedroom in the past has been an area where those crazy conversations would take place, stop now. Here is why:

Our minds are transformed and renewed (Romans 12) and sometimes that transformation is not a positive transformation. When our minds go to a place mentally where we have turned our bedrooms into a "principal's office", meaning "this is where I get called on the carpet"... "this is where the other shoe drops"...this creates an inability to celebrate your oneness (physically) through the One. Our minds have turned this into a place of doom versus a place of worship...hahaha, yes we said worship. God created sex; therefore it is good when celebrated in the manner that brings Him glory. This can be a place of fireworks, a place of nooorahs...a place to celebrate!

You are now equipped to move through conversations in a healthy manner. Remember, your marriage has its own DNA, therefore trust the One who brought you together to navigate you through life thus keeping you in the sacred space of your common ground

Chapter 9
Tools to help you along the way

Debby and I get to read some great books. <u>For Women Only</u> and <u>For Men Only</u> by Shaunti Feldhaun are ones that helped us big time in the early stages of us learning to chat with each other versus at each other. You may have them on your shelves. If so, go dust them and go through them or if you haven't already gone through them we have a way for you to cruise through the books that is empowering.

Ladies, you read the book that the men read (for men only) and highlight the areas in the book that pertain to you, with any notes surrounding the areas highlighted. Write "yes" by items that pertain to you, write "no" by others that don't.

Men, you read the book that the girls read (for women only) and do the same. Highlight the areas that pertain to you, with any notes surrounding the areas highlighted…place yes by items, place no by others…

Allow yourselves to coach one another up in how God wired you. Neither of you is a mind reader, yet you sure do want the other one to be able to do so.

Once you have highlighted the books hand them to each other and cruise through. This will give you the chance to look under the hood a bit. What this also does is give those who are a bit reserved in sharing how they really feel a chance to have a voice.

You will definitely have some "Really? Are you serious? Wow, I never knew that!" moments as you read.

Other books that are beneficial:

- <u>The Five Love Languages</u> by Gary Chapman
- <u>Wild at Heart</u> by John Eldredge (I recommend women to read this especially if you have boys in the house)
- <u>Captivating</u> by John and Stasi Eldredge

- <u>Waking the Dead</u> by John Eldredge
- <u>Love and Respect</u> by Dr. Emmerson Eggriches
- <u>Boundaries</u> by Henry Cloud and John Townsend
- <u>Codependent No More</u> by Melody Beattie
- <u>Sacred Marriage</u> by Gary Thomas
- <u>Heart Made Whole</u> by Christa Black Gifford

Some other folks I (Mike) love: Neil Anderson, Henri Nouwen, Brennan Manning, Bob George, Phillip Yancey, and Jean Vanier. There are many others, yet these are the frequent "return to" guys. They serve as mentors in our life in how they pour themselves out on the pages.

CONCLUSION & APPLICATION

You can read and read and read and read, but the application of what you are reading is when results/changes occur.

Ever read the instructions on a shampoo bottle?

Pour…lather…rinse…repeat

It's the same concept:

- Stay in a state of repeating what you have learned about each other. Remain in a mode of discovery of one another through how you communicate with each other.
- Make sure the words you express match the body language given and that his or her definition of your words lines up with your definition…
- Remind each other that you are for one another, meaning you want and desire the best for each other.
- Stop, drop, and pray when the fur on your neck stands up.
- Take a timeout.
- Ask yourself "What and who am I defending and why?"
- Repeat.

We hope these pages are helpful. One last resource for you. You are welcome to send us an email and we will help coach you along the road between the 700 hundred fence posts to gain that ground where you both give a little because "there ain't no road too long when we meet in the middle."

mbivins@therefugemboro.com
www.therefugemboro.com

You are loved!

1. Diamond Rio. Meet in the Middle. Arista, 1991. CD.
2. "National Marriage and Divorce Rate Trends." Centers for Disease Control and Prevention. Centers for Disease Control and Prevention, 19 Feb. 2015. Web. 11 Nov. 2015.
3. Thompson, Jeff, Ph.D. "Is Nonverbal Communication a Numbers Game?" Psychology Today. Is Nonverbal Communication a Numbers Game?, n.d. Web. 11 Nov. 2015.
4. Dictionary.com. Dictionary.com, n.d. Web. 11 Nov. 2015.
5. (All Scripture References)
6. Holy Bible: New Living Translation. Wheaton, IL: Tyndale House, 1996. Print.

CPSIA information can be obtained
at www.ICGtesting.com
Printed in the USA
LVHW061336070723
751708LV00044B/1066